A gift for

....

From

....

Date

....

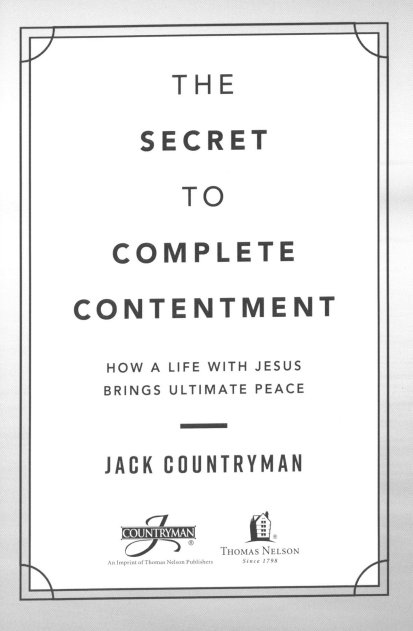

THE

SECRET

TO

COMPLETE

CONTENTMENT

HOW A LIFE WITH JESUS
BRINGS ULTIMATE PEACE

—

JACK COUNTRYMAN

COUNTRYMAN®

An Imprint of Thomas Nelson Publishers

THOMAS NELSON®
Since 1798

Published in Nashville, Tennessee, by Thomas Nelson. Thomas Nelson is a registered trademark of HarperCollins Christian Publishing, Inc.

Thomas Nelson titles may be purchased in bulk for educational, business, fund-raising, or sales promotional use. For information, please email SpecialMarkets@ThomasNelson.com.

Unless otherwise noted, Scripture quotations are from the New King James Version®. Copyright © 1982 by Thomas Nelson. Used by permission. All rights reserved.

Scripture quotations marked AMP are from the Amplified Bible (AMP). Copyright © 2015 by The Lockman Foundation. Used by permission. www.Lockman.org

Scripture quotations marked NIV are from the Holy Bible, New International Version®, NIV®. Copyright © 1973, 1978, 1984, 2011 by Biblica, Inc.® Used by permission of Zondervan. All rights reserved worldwide. www.zondervan.com. The "NIV" and "New International Version" are trademarks registered in the United States Patent and Trademark Office by Biblica, Inc.®

Any internet addresses, phone numbers, or company or product information printed in this book are offered as a resource and are not intended in any way to be or to imply an endorsement by Thomas Nelson, nor does Thomas Nelson vouch for the existence, content, or services of these sites, phone numbers, companies, or products beyond the life of this book.

Cover designed by Jonathan Maloney
Interior design by Kristy Edwards

ISBN 978-1-4002-4228-3 (audiobook)
ISBN 978-1-4002-4227-6 (eBook)
ISBN 978-1-4002-4225-2 (HC)

Printed in Malaysia

24 25 26 27 28 OFF 10 9 8 7 6 5 4 3 2 1

CONTENTS

INTRODUCTION

I f someone asked you, "What brings you contentment?" I bet you and I would have similar answers. Who doesn't want good health, a wonderful spouse, amazing kids, friends who love us, a great house, a cool car, success in the workplace, and money in the bank? Yet if we were to acquire these things, we wouldn't feel content at all—because we'd still want more (and if we're honest with ourselves, we often just want more than the people in our circle have!).

The secret to complete contentment is not found in any of those things. In fact, the Amplified Bible says real contentment "comes from a sense of inner confidence based on the sufficiency of God" (1 Timothy 6:6 AMP). The hunger for the peace of mind that God has placed within us—for contentment—can be satisfied only by a relationship with Jesus Christ.

If you don't already have a relationship with

Jesus, know that He is waiting for you to welcome Him into your life.

Rest assured that Jesus will never force Himself on you or me, but if we invite Him in, He will fill us with His Spirit who will guide our steps, grow our faith, offer comfort, and pray for us. The Spirit will help each of us know the peace and contentment that God wants us to experience. And so will Scripture.

In fact, my desire is that God will use this book to open your heart to the life-changing and empowering truth of His Word. May the truth you find in the Bible—which I quote in these pages—kindle a desire to live in the center of God's will. And may the gift of His presence show you all that He created you to be.

And as you read, remember: living in the love of Jesus is the secret to complete contentment.

1

FROM THE INSIDE OUT

The law of the LORD is perfect,
converting the soul;
The testimony of the LORD is sure,
making wise the simple;
The statutes of the LORD are
right, rejoicing the heart;
The commandment of the LORD is
pure, enlightening the eyes. . . .
Let the words of my mouth and
the meditation of my heart
Be acceptable in Your sight,
O LORD, my strength and my Redeemer.
PSALM 19:7–8, 14

When you read these verses from Psalm 19, you may notice that David referred to God's Word in four ways: as His *law, testimony, statutes,* and *commandment.* Maybe you noticed how David described God's Word: *perfect, sure, right,* and *pure.* Be sure to note the transformative, from-the-inside-out work God does through Scripture. That work is key to knowing contentment.

The Bible contains words that—by the power of the Holy Spirit—transform our soul, make us wise, bring us joy, and increase our understanding. We experience this transforming power as we read, learn, and live according to God's principles and instructions. Using the truth of the Bible, the Holy Spirit can renew our mind, change our perspective, align our values with God's, free us from unhelpful alliances to the things of this world, and give us His perspective on what matters.

God also uses His powerful Word and the presence of His Holy Spirit at work within us to help us speak words and have thoughts that are acceptable in His sight.

As you journey through life with Him, God enables you to know contentment. One way to receive that gift is by spending time studying the Bible and yielding your heart and mind to the Spirit's work. God will transform you into a contented person, and He'll do so from the inside out.

Holy Spirit, thank You for the from-the-inside-out work You are doing in my heart so I can be God's light, walk in His wisdom, and know the blessing of contentment.

2

TRUST IN THE LORD

Trust in the Lord with all your heart,
And lean not on your own understanding;
In all your ways acknowledge Him,
And He shall direct your paths.
PROVERBS 3:5–6

n your life, what is contentment's greatest enemy? For many of us, it's our tendency to worry. It comes naturally to us, and because our Creator God knows that, He tells us to not worry. Here in Proverbs 3, He states it more positively as He sets forth a solution—one that is simple but not easy.

"Trust in the Lord" is both God's call to not worry and the better option He gives us to move forward. He invites us to trust Him with the pressures of today and our fears about tomorrow. And He asks us to trust in Him with all our heart.

We can, for instance, trust with all our mind that the chair we are sitting in will hold up under our weight. We show our wholehearted trust in that chair's ability to hold us when we actually sit in it. We can believe with all our mind that God will direct our path, but we believe with all our heart when we actually seek His will, listen in prayer for His words of direction, and choose to focus our thoughts on Him. Reminding ourselves of who God is—almighty, wise, merciful, loving, gracious, faithful, and compassionate—will fuel our trust in Him.

Are you willing to let this Lord lead you moment by moment "in all your ways"? God wants us to trust Him completely, and we demonstrate our trust when we let Him guide our life. We find contentment as we walk along the path He has for us.

> Lord, please grow my trust in You by helping me recognize Your guiding voice and giving me courage to walk the path You have for me, a path where I will know contentment in You.

3

WHOSE CONTENTMENT?

Trust in the LORD, and do good;
Dwell in the land, and feed on His faithfulness.
PSALM 37:3

oing good to others—doesn't that suggest we'd be increasing *their* contentment rather than our own? I propose that in this case, contentment is not a matter of either/or but of both/and.

After all, as the apostle Paul quoted Jesus, "It is more blessed to give than to receive" (Acts 20:35). "Doing good" implies giving, but not only gifts that are tangible. We can give a shoulder to lean on and an ear to listen. We can pray for people, even if they aren't aware of it. We can take a meal, leave a bag of groceries on the porch, or watch the kids on a Saturday. We can drive people to appointments, vacuum their house, or mow their lawn. We can cover a rental payment or help with some bills.

And we can do good generously and frequently when we "trust in the Lord." As we seek to obey Him and to be His light, He will lead us to people we can bless with our help and provision. Remembering His past faithfulness and knowing that our unchanging God will always be faithful, we can help people. When we do good, we make our Lord's love more real to those we love in His name.

Whatever good we offer, when we do good to others, our true Christian self shows up. We will find deep satisfaction in serving people God puts in our path and showing them the selfless love that points people to Jesus. God blesses us so that we can be a blessing to those around us. Being used by God truly brings genuine contentment.

Good and gracious God, thank You for the contentment I know when You use me to bless others in ways that make Your goodness and grace more real to them.

4

GOD'S PLEASURE IN OUR PURPOSE

"I am the vine, you are the branches. He who abides in Me, and I in him, bears much fruit; for without Me you can do nothing."
JOHN 15:5

reated to swim, a fish swept onto dry sand can't be what God made it to be. Created to fly, a bird locked in a cage can't experience the soaring-above-the-earth freedom God made it to know. Created to abide in Jesus, the Vine, you and I can't bear the fruit God made us to bear when we are living apart from Him.

But what does a life of abiding in Jesus even look like? Simply put, it is a life yielded completely to God. We live focused on Him, filled with His Holy Spirit, willing to go wherever He leads and to do whatever He calls us to do. Living aligned with our Creator God enables us to know purpose, meaning, and joy.

Knowing our purpose on this planet—being salt and light, loving with Jesus' love, sharing the gospel—and living out that purpose brings profound satisfaction and peace. One might even say contentment. Jesus clarified: "As the branch cannot bear fruit of itself, unless it abides in the vine, neither can you, unless you abide in Me" (v. 4).

So if we want to bear fruit—if we want to live out our purpose on this planet and find meaning in life—we need to abide in Jesus, relying on Him to guide our steps and being filled with His love so that we may share it with others.

Maybe you've heard the quote from the movie *Chariots of Fire*, where the actor playing Olympic runner Eric Liddell said, "God made me fast. And when I run, I feel His pleasure." Feeling God's pleasure is surely an aspect of knowing contentment.

Lord God, please help me to know not only Your pleasure but also heaven-sent contentment as, abiding in You, I bear kingdom fruit where You have planted me.

5

STEPPING TOWARD CONTENTMENT

Rejoice in the Lord always. Again I will say, rejoice! . . . Be anxious for nothing, but in everything by prayer and supplication, with thanksgiving, let your requests be made known to God; and the peace of God, which surpasses all understanding, will guard your hearts and minds through Christ Jesus.
PHILIPPIANS 4:4, 6–7

Rejoice in the Lord" is a call to rejoice in all that Jesus is and in all that He has done. For starters, we can rejoice in the fact that our Lord Jesus is loving, gracious, patient, compassionate, forgiving, faithful, and good. We can rejoice in the amazing grace of His dying on the cross for our sins, redeeming us from separation from God, offering us hope for today and for eternity, and blessing us with His Spirit. Despite all that Jesus is and all that He has done and continues to do for us, we still need the reminder to "rejoice in [Him]."

And Paul, the author of Philippians, went on to offer tips for living with a mindfulness of our many reasons to rejoice. We are, for instance, to pray with thanksgiving. Having placed our concerns at Jesus' feet, we will then know His peace. Paul also called us to take charge of our thought life. Are we filling our minds with ideas that fuel joy or worry, calm or stress, hope or hopelessness? Paul wisely counseled us to keep our minds focused on "whatever things are true . . . noble . . . just . . . pure . . . lovely . . . of good report . . . [and] praiseworthy" (v. 8).

Choosing to think on the things of God and

committing our problems to the Lord, we can rest in His care. Acknowledging His faithfulness and love will fuel joy and hope—and a good amount of contentment—whatever life's circumstances.

Please teach me to live, Almighty God, with a more consistent focus on You, surrendering my problems to You, resting in Your faithful care, and knowing contentment in the joy and hope You provide.

6

THE SAME YESTERDAY, TODAY, AND FOREVER

I know the thoughts that I think toward you, says the LORD, thoughts of peace and not of evil, to give you a future and a hope. Then you will call upon Me and go and pray to Me, and I will listen to you. And you will seek Me and find Me, when you search for Me with all your heart. I will be found by you, says the LORD.
JEREMIAH 29:11–14

Prophets of the Old Testament stood before God's people with messages from Him, and today's passage is one example. Jeremiah was speaking to the nation of Israel, and the God he spoke of is the same today as He was then. Our unchanging God is also unchanging in His gift-giving. Just as He blessed Israel with His grace and mercy, He will bless us with His grace and mercy today.

So consider Jeremiah's prophetic words of hope. Speaking for God, Jeremiah told Israel that He wants to give them "a future and a hope." Jeremiah reassured Israel that God will listen when His people call on Him and pray to Him. Ultimately, God gave His people a future and hope—a heavenly future and eternal hope—through His crucified and resurrected Son. Jesus bridged the gap between holy God and sinful us, so we can not only call on God but call Him "*Abba*, Father" when we do. Clearly, God's Old Testament promise stands: we find Him when we seek Him with all our heart.

Our unchanging Lord—who is the same yesterday, today, and forever—offers you hope for the future, His promise to listen when you pray, and His pledge that when you seek Him, you will find Him. Rest in those truths and know contentment.

Thank You for the peace, hope, and, yes, contentment that I experience when I remember that You, my gracious, merciful, faithful, and attentive Father God, are the same yesterday, today, and forever.

7

THE GOOD SHEPHERD

"I am the good shepherd. The good shepherd gives His life for the sheep. But a hireling, he who is not the shepherd, one who does not own the sheep, sees the wolf coming and leaves the sheep and flees; and the wolf catches the sheep and scatters them. The hireling flees because he is a hireling and does not care about the sheep. I am the good shepherd; and I know My sheep, and am known by My own. As the Father knows Me, even so I know the Father; and I lay down My life for the sheep."
JOHN 10:11–15

Not many of us in the twenty-first century appreciate all that a shepherd does for his sheep. His or her role as protector and provider is multifaceted and demanding. Leading the flock to clean water and fresh pasture, protecting the sheep from predators as well as ear mites, searching for lost sheep, standing upright the sheep that stumble—the shepherd is on duty 24/7 overseeing the very needy charges.

Jesus is our Good Shepherd who watches over us, His vulnerable, frequently straying sheep. Going beyond a first-century shepherd whose life could be endangered by wolves and lions that saw sheep as their next meal, our Good Shepherd came to earth to give His life to save us. He died an excruciating death on the cross as the perfect and therefore final sacrifice for our sins, so that we might know God's forgiveness and eternal life with Him.

Why would we ever think we could find a better life outside the care of our Good Shepherd?

Thank You, Jesus, for being my Good Shepherd—for helping me stand when I fall, overseeing my care 24/7, and coming after me when, foolishly looking for contentment apart from You, I stray.

8

IF GOD IS FOR US

If God is for us, who can be against us? . . .
Who shall separate us from the love of Christ?
Shall tribulation, or distress, or persecution, or
famine, or nakedness, or peril, or sword? . . .
I am persuaded that neither death nor life,
nor angels nor principalities nor powers,
nor things present nor things to come, nor
height nor depth, nor any other created thing,
shall be able to separate us from the love of
God which is in Christ Jesus our Lord.
ROMANS 8:31, 35, 38–39

Did you really hear—with your heart as well as your head—the words you just read? Or are these remarkable statements so familiar that you nod along rather than sit in awe of the profound truth they set forth?

"If God is for us, who can be against us?" This question points to the unshakable security and hope we can find in the love God offers us, a love made manifest in Jesus' death on the cross. What a testimony, that God is indeed for us. The trouble and pain we all experience may call into question whether God is on our side, but a glance at the cross reassures us that He is.

If we need any more convincing, in verses 38 through 39 Paul listed the forces we may believe could separate us from God's love, and he declared that could never be the case. Once we accept Jesus' death on the cross for our sin—once we embrace that act as the rock-solid testimony of God's love for us—absolutely nothing can break that bond of divine, life-saving love. We are secure in the arms of Jesus, today and forevermore. Could anything in all creation make us any more content?

Creator God, You know how I long for security, and I thank You for providing it in the love Jesus revealed on the cross.

9

ETERNAL LIFE
HAS BEGUN

*He who has the Son has life; he who does
not have the Son of God does not have life.
These things I have written to you who
believe in the name of the Son of God, that
you may know that you have eternal life.*
1 JOHN 5:12–13

The moment we accept Jesus as our Savior and Lord, our eternal life with Him begins. In other words, our eternal life has already begun.

We don't have to wait to see His glory: we get glimpses of it as the heavens make their own declaration in starry nights and brilliant sunsets (Psalm 19:1).

We don't need to wait to experience His unconditional love: we get tastes of it through His people.

We don't have to wait for heaven to know His forgiveness and grace: the written Word declares that He is faithful to forgive our sins when we confess them (1 John 1:9).

We definitely don't need to wait to start worshipping God: throughout the psalms, the writers invite us to celebrate our glorious God with music and praise.

When we declare our faith in Jesus, we receive His Spirit, who works in us to make us more like Jesus, as we anticipate spending the majority of our eternal life in the presence of our heavenly Father and in the company of our Savior.

May these truths about eternity in the present bring you joy and peace.

Thank You that my eternal life with You has already begun, that I can already know the contentment of seeing Your glory, experiencing Your love, and rejoicing in Your presence.

10

BEING LED IN THE
WAY EVERLASTING

Where can I go from Your Spirit?
Or where can I flee from Your presence? . . .
If I take the wings of the morning,
And dwell in the uttermost parts of the sea,
Even there Your hand shall lead me,
And Your right hand shall hold me. . . .
Search me, O God, and know my heart;
Try me, and know my anxieties;
And see if there is any wicked way in me,
And lead me in the way everlasting.
PSALM 139:7, 9–10, 23–24

How great is our God: all-knowing, all-powerful, and present everywhere! We cannot escape the presence of the Lord. If that sounds a bit frightening, remember that He is the One who "formed [your] inward parts" and knit you together "in [your] mother's womb" (Psalm 139:13). He wrote in His book all "the days fashioned for [you], when as yet there were none of them" (v. 16).

God didn't create you and leave you on your own. As we've seen, He is with you always, wanting you to be blessed by an intimate relationship with Him. Understanding that, the psalmist asked the Lord to reveal his worries and "wicked way" so that nothing would stand between him and his Creator. The psalmist also wisely turned to God, ready to follow wholeheartedly the One who would "lead [him] in the way everlasting."

Like the psalmist, may we marvel that we are "fearfully and wonderfully made" (v. 14), that the Lord is always present with us, and that He longs to lead us on His good path for us. May we be fully content, knowing that we were created by our loving

31

God, relying on His presence with us, and trusting in His leading.

What glorious reasons for contentment, Lord God! You created me, You are always with me, and I can trust in Your leading. Thank You, my good and gracious God!

11

SCRIPTURE'S LIFE-CHANGING TRUTH

The word of God is living and powerful, and sharper than any two-edged sword, piercing even to the division of soul and spirit, and of joints and marrow, and is a discerner of the thoughts and intents of the heart.

HEBREWS 4:12

As we read the life-transforming truths of Scripture, we realize that our gracious God "has given to us all things that pertain to life and godliness" (2 Peter 1:3). We learn why we need a Savior, and we see that Jesus perfectly meets the requirements to be that Savior. We also learn what it means to live with Jesus as our Lord and how the gift of His own Holy Spirit within us enables us to do so.

The Word of God shows us not only the way of life that will glorify God but also the ways we fall short from living that way. Used by the Spirit, this "living and powerful" Word reveals the sometimes-harsh truth about the nature of our thoughts and the intentions of our heart. Knowing this information, we can repent of our sinful ways and live freely in relationship with our God. The Spirit also helps us apply God's Word to our lives so that our thoughts, words, and deeds glorify Him.

Through the gift of God's written Word, we learn what it means to be His child, living in relationship with Him. As we follow the Bible's road map, we see that Jesus desires us to walk through each day with a keen awareness of His life-giving presence with us. Abiding in God's Word and living each day in His presence enable us to know His blessings of peace and contentment.

Thank You, Holy Spirit, for not letting me settle for false contentment. By showing me ways I fall short, You protect me from being content in my sin so that I can know far better contentment in You.

12

LOVING IN GOD'S POWER AND FOR HIS GLORY

Above all things have fervent love for one another, for "love will cover a multitude of sins." Be hospitable to one another without grumbling. As each one has received a gift, minister it to one another, as good stewards of the manifold grace of God.
1 PETER 4:8–10

n this passage, God clearly calls us to share our love for Him with others—especially in the realm of hospitality.

What would loving others in this way look like? Think about the times you have been sincerely loved and welcomed by someone who was very aware of your shortcomings and sins. Bestow that life-giving blessing when you "have fervent love for one another."

To whom might you offer hospitality? Think beyond the circle of "your people" who might return the favor. Even when it costs you not only money but also time, wisdom, emotions, and patience, extend that hospitality with a willing and cheerful spirit.

And if you haven't already, identify the gifts for ministry God has given you. God didn't bless you with talents and interests merely to keep them to yourself. He wants you to use those gifts for the good of His people so "that in all things God may be glorified" (v. 11).

Yet as we love, extend hospitality, and use our gifts among God's people, things will go wrong. What do we do then? We keep loving people with

God's love. We let God's love for them flow through us, despite their sinful or merely annoying ways.

Doing all that God calls us to do—that's primarily loving others—brings us a life of contentment. Try it and see for yourself!

I know, Lord, that living life Your way brings contentment. So may I know the contentment that comes as You enable me to, in obedience, extend hospitality and love.

13

TRUST, DELIGHT,
COMMIT, AND REST

Trust in the LORD, and do good. . . .
Delight yourself also in the LORD. . . .
Commit your way to the LORD. . . .
Rest in the LORD, and wait patiently for Him.
PSALM 37:3–5, 7

Psalm 37 celebrates the blessings God has for the righteous. But in this psalm, David also outlined a path to an additional blessing: knowing contentment in this life.

First, God calls us to "trust in the LORD" for our good. We can know peace when we choose to put our faith in Him instead of worrying, trying to do life on our own, or solely counting on fellow human beings. Without peace rooted in our knowledge that God is gracious, generous, and faithful, we can't know contentment, no matter our possessions and accomplishments.

Next, God invites us to "delight yourself also in the LORD." Delighting in God can be as unique as the person doing the delighting. Surfers delight in God's oceans; skiers, in His mountains. New parents delight in the miracle of childbirth; songwriters, in their polished creation. And all of us can delight in God's Word and in getting to know Him better. Delight fuels contentment.

David also called us to "commit your way to the LORD." Surrendering our very life to God and yielding to His good and perfect will open us to blessings from God: blessings of direction, protection, and provision greater than we can even imagine. And having committed ourselves to God, we can then "rest in the LORD, and wait patiently for Him." Once in the care of our heavenly Father, we can know perfect rest.

When we trust in the Lord, delight in Him, commit our life to Him, and rest in Him, we are able to know contentment whatever life's circumstances.

Trusting in You, delighting in You, committing my way to You, resting in You—please keep me on this path that leads to peace, joy, and contentment in You!

14

GLORY TO GOD FOR HIS GRACE!

I was formerly a blasphemer, a persecutor, and an insolent man; but I obtained mercy because I did it ignorantly in unbelief. And the grace of our Lord was exceedingly abundant, with faith and love which are in Christ Jesus. This is a faithful saying and worthy of all acceptance, that Christ Jesus came into the world to save sinners, of whom I am chief.
1 TIMOTHY 1:13–15

When we human beings actually acknowledge our sin, we often comfort ourselves by making comparisons: "Yes, I'm a sinner—but at least my sin isn't as bad as *that* person's!" In 1 Timothy 1, though, we hear Paul doing the opposite: he declared that *he* was the chief of all sinners.

As a former relentless persecutor of the Christian church, Paul could make a good case for his assertion, but clearly, God redeemed this so-called chief sinner. By the time of this writing, Paul had turned away from his former way of life and now preached the "exceedingly abundant" grace, faith, and love of Jesus Christ. Few people have preached the forgiveness and love of Christ with more heartfelt passion than the rescued and transformed Paul.

What amazes me about Paul is his unapologetic description of himself. He unashamedly confessed his heinous sin of persecuting innocent Christians, and he let everyone know that he had been saved by God's grace. Like Paul, we can confess our sin, turn from it, and proclaim with him, "To the King eternal, immortal, invisible, to God who alone is wise, be honor and glory forever and ever. Amen" (v. 17). And we'll be well on the way to genuine contentment. Glory to God for His grace!

Thank You for Your grace that rescued me from sin and continues to transform me. May You receive the glory for changing my heart, for making me more like Jesus, and for blessing me with contentment whatever life's circumstances.

15

SELFLESS AND SACRIFICIAL LOVE

*Present your bodies a living sacrifice, holy,
acceptable to God, which is your reasonable
service. And do not be conformed to this world,
but be transformed by the renewing of your
mind, that you may prove what is that good
and acceptable and perfect will of God. . . .
Let love be without hypocrisy. . . . Be kindly
affectionate to one another with brotherly love,
in honor giving preference to one another.*
ROMANS 12:1–2, 9–10

The apostle Paul called us to present ourselves to God as living sacrifices, yielding to Him our hearts and asking Him to use us for His glory and for the good of His people. We also offer God our mind, relying on Him to help us stand against the world's influences and allow His Spirit to align our thinking with kingdom values.

Wanting to obey Him, we act according to "that good and acceptable and perfect will of God." We start, for instance, to love people with His love. Christlike, selfless love is sacrificial love, especially when the people God puts in our path are hard to love. Furthermore, the choice to love is the choice to give up time and money. It's the choice to serve by listening and praying, silently or aloud. In Philippians, Paul defined this kind of brotherly love: "Esteem others better than [yourselves]. Let each of you look out not only for his own interests, but also for the interests of others" (2:3–4).

Clearly, the choice to love is a choice to give up your plans, desires, and preferences. Yet, somewhat paradoxically, you'll find that this kind of selfless, sacrificial love opens the door to genuine contentment.

May I experience more fully the contentment that comes with choosing to love, dying to myself, and yielding my plans, desires, and preferences to Your good and perfect will for me.

16

DRAWING NEAR
TO GOD

*Having boldness to enter the Holiest by the
blood of Jesus, . . . let us draw near with a
true heart in full assurance of faith, having
our hearts sprinkled from an evil conscience
and our bodies washed with pure water.
Let us hold fast the confession of our hope
without wavering, for He who promised is
faithful. And let us consider one another
in order to stir up love and good works.*
HEBREWS 10:19, 22–24

t is finished," Jesus said from the cross (John 19:30). He, the sinless Lamb of God, had died as the perfect and forever sacrifice for our sins. Three days later, proving Himself victorious over both sin and death, the resurrected Jesus secured our salvation. We who have put our faith in the slain and risen Jesus and received forgiveness for our sins are therefore able to "draw near [to our holy God] . . . in full assurance of faith."

As we draw near to God, He uses our life experiences to make us more like our Savior and Lord. By the power of the Holy Spirit, God enables us to become more like Jesus, better able to shine His light, share His love, speak the gospel truth about Him, and serve Him in any context. We can "draw near" to God confident that He will enable us to love, to serve, and to do "good works" for His glory.

We can also be confident that God will use trials to grow our faith and use our interactions with other believers to refine our faith the way iron sharpens iron. We can rest content that God will not waste pain and hardship as He makes those of us who are saved by faith more like His Son.

Lord, You don't waste pain, but instead, You use it to help us shine more brightly, love more sincerely, speak the gospel more boldly, and serve more wholeheartedly, all the while being blessed by contentment in You.

17

GOD'S GRACE TO
THE HUMBLE

*"God resists the proud,
But gives grace to the humble."*

*Therefore submit to God. Resist the devil
and he will flee from you. Draw near to God
and He will draw near to you. Cleanse your
hands, you sinners; and purify your hearts,
you double-minded. . . . Humble yourselves in
the sight of the Lord, and He will lift you up.*
JAMES 4:6–8, 10

Have you ever wondered why God wants us to ask Him for the things He already knows we need? I think the reason is relationship. He created us to be in relationship with Him, and wanting our needs met is one reason for us to go to Him whose arms are always open wide to His children.

So why don't we readily go to God with our needs, worries, pain, weakness, and fear? The issue may be our pride. We human beings can be so falsely confident of ourselves that we have no room in our life for Jesus. Or we can be guilty of the false truth that says we have made so many bad decisions and committed so many grave sins that God could never forgive us, so we stay away from Him.

But consider the wonderful promise of verse 8: "Draw near to God and He will draw near to you." Whether humbled by our awareness of our need, our limitations, or our bad choices—or by an awareness of God in His goodness, grace, and holiness—we must take the first step toward Him by humbling ourselves. Making room for God in our lives is a position of humility that God honors:

He receives us and blesses us with all we need and more, including a blessed contentment.

Almighty God, help me to live with my eyes fixed on holy and glorious You so that I remain humble, blessed by Your grace and the contentment of living as Your beloved child.

18

PEACE AND GRATITUDE, LOVE AND CONTENTMENT

As the elect of God, holy and beloved, put on tender mercies, kindness, humility, meekness, longsuffering; bearing with one another, and forgiving one another. . . . Above all these things put on love, which is the bond of perfection. And let the peace of God rule in your hearts . . . and be thankful. . . . Whatever you do in word or deed, do all in the name of the Lord Jesus, giving thanks to God the Father through Him.

COLOSSIANS 3:12–15, 17

Mercy, kindness, humility, patience, forgiveness—we can't make ourselves live out any of these traits simply by wanting to! Thankfully, Paul called us to "put on" these traits, meaning they are provided for us by Someone. That Someone is the Holy Spirit, who works in each of us to make us more the person God wants us to be. Only with the Spirit's transforming power can we know peace, extend love, and live with gratitude.

Yet I think that we human beings want desperately to know the peace of God that comes only after we have peace *with* God. Knowing peace *with* God is possible only because Jesus' death on the cross bridged the unbridgeable gap between holy God and sinful humanity. We know the peace of God only after we surrender and allow Him to be the Lord and Master of our lives—and there is no downside to that decision.

In fact, when we have surrendered to God, we can more freely choose to "do all [that we do and say] in the name of the Lord Jesus, giving thanks to God the Father through Him." Gratitude not only fuels gratitude. A thankful heart means joy and contentment as well.

Lord, You call me to put on mercy, kindness, humility, patience, and forgiveness. Thank You for enabling me to do exactly that—and then blessing me with contentment as well.

19

BY GRACE . . . THROUGH FAITH

God, who is rich in mercy, because of His great love with which He loved us, even when we were dead in trespasses, made us alive together with Christ (by grace you have been saved), and raised us up together, and made us sit together in the heavenly places in Christ Jesus. . . . For by grace you have been saved through faith, and that not of yourselves; it is the gift of God, not of works, lest anyone should boast.

EPHESIANS 2:4–6, 8–9

Knowing the "bad news" tends to make the "good news" sweeter.

The bad news is all of us "have sinned and fall short of the glory of God" (Romans 3:23). Before we knew Jesus, each one of us was dead and lost in our sin.

Now the good news: "by grace you have been saved through faith" (v. 8). Notice that Paul didn't say, "You have been saved by good deeds, kind words, generous financial gifts, start-up philanthropies, or converting your quota of souls." Instead, Paul stated the simple truth: you have been saved by God's grace.

Grace is a churchy word that means "gift." In other words, we can't earn our holy God's forgiveness of our sin; we simply receive it. Acting on His immeasurable love, God freely gives us salvation.

Oh, God knows us from the inside out, and He loves us despite our faults and mistakes. In His grace, He sees us dressed in Jesus' robes of righteousness, cleansed and forgiven, even as He patiently molds our character and guides our steps for His glory, for our good—and for our contentment.

Just as darkness makes light seem brighter, the bad news of my sin makes the good news of Your grace sweeter. Thank You not only for the grace of Your forgiveness but also for the gift of contentment in You.

20

THE CHEERFUL GIVER

He who sows sparingly will also reap sparingly, and he who sows bountifully will also reap bountifully. So let each one give as he purposes in his heart, not grudgingly or of necessity; for God loves a cheerful giver. And God is able to make all grace abound toward you, that you, always having all sufficiency in all things, may have an abundance for every good work.
2 CORINTHIANS 9:6–8

What was the best gift you've ever received? Now think about the best gift you've ever given. Which event brought more joy and greater contentment? I bet it was the act of giving.

God Himself finds great joy in giving. Consider that He takes care of us and, by His grace, daily sustains us. God provides the air we breathe, the food we eat, the water we drink, and this indescribably beautiful world we live in. He gave us His Son, the Son gave us His Spirit, and His Spirit oversaw the production and preservation of Scripture, which guides our steps in daily living.

Created in God's image, we, too, have the ability to give because He gives to us abundantly. Besides, everything we own belongs to Him anyway. We are simply stewards of all the time, treasure, and talent He has entrusted to us.

The Lord has given us people to love and people who love us in return. So may we give cheerfully, even when our giving stretches us and tests our faith, trusting that He will indeed continue to provide for us. And may we savor those times when our giving brings the warm contentment of knowing we have pleased our God.

Forgive me, Lord, when I struggle to share what You've given me. Help me to know contentment in Your abundant provision and then—in faith—be a generous steward of my time, treasure, and talent.

21

OUR WEAKNESS, GOD'S STRENGTH

A thorn in the flesh was given to me, a messenger of Satan to buffet me, lest I be exalted above measure. Concerning this thing I pleaded with the Lord three times that it might depart from me. And He said to me, "My grace is sufficient for you, for My strength is made perfect in weakness." . . . Therefore I take pleasure in infirmities, in reproaches, in needs, in persecutions, in distresses, for Christ's sake. For when I am weak, then I am strong.
2 CORINTHIANS 12:7–10

Before his conversion, the apostle Paul was "breathing threats and murder against the disciples of the Lord" (Acts 9:1). A few verses later we read that he encountered the resurrected Jesus.

In an instant, the enemy of upstart Christianity was on his way to becoming an apologist and unequaled preacher. Paul's faithfulness to Jesus, though, meant hardship and persecution. The list of his sufferings for Jesus includes shipwrecks, beatings, imprisonment, hunger, and cold (2 Corinthians 11:23–28). But on one point of suffering, Paul was vague: he never identified the thorn in his flesh.

With his stellar education, the respect he knew as a Pharisee, and his enviable encounter with Jesus, Paul knew that pride was a real possibility. Its presence could cloud his presentation of the gospel and undermine his effectiveness for the Lord. So as much as he wanted to be rid of that thorn, Paul appreciated its value: it kept him from being "exalted above measure." Instead, he relied on Jesus for the grace and strength he needed to continue his ministry.

When life's thorns prompt us to turn to the Lord, may we find contentment as well as strength and peace. Our gracious God doesn't waste pain: He has a good purpose for everything we face.

You, gracious God, who bring beauty from ashes, can of course help me know strength in weakness, hope when suffering comes, and contentment despite thorns. Thank You.

22

CRUCIFIED WITH CHRIST

We who are Jews by nature . . . knowing that a man is not justified by the works of the law but by faith in Jesus Christ, even we have believed in Christ Jesus, that we might be justified by faith in Christ and not by the works of the law; for by the works of the law no flesh shall be justified. . . .

I have been crucified with Christ; it is no longer I who live, but Christ lives in me; and the life which I now live in the flesh I live by faith in the Son of God, who loved me and gave Himself for me.
GALATIANS 2:15–16, 20

We are justified not by any effort on our part—only when we put our faith in Jesus, who paid the price for our sin. Our holy God regards us as forgiven and righteous, freeing us to proclaim like Paul, "I have been crucified with Christ . . . and the life which I now live in the flesh I live by faith in the Son of God."

Being "crucified with Christ" means our sins are forgiven, and we are free to enjoy a relationship with God. In fact, living as a follower of Jesus means allowing God, through His Spirit, to live *in* us and *through* us. It means yielding to the Holy Spirit's guiding, transforming, and refining work in our life.

With the Holy Spirit dwelling in us, we have all the power we need to resist temptation, to step out in faith when God calls, and to represent the Lord with our words and deeds.

And by the power of the Holy Spirit within us, we can know the contentment that comes with saying no to sin and yes to God as we place our trust in Him.

I praise You, God, that You forgive my sins and that You have provided the Holy Spirit to help me when temptation arises. Thank You for the contentment of being in this grace-filled relationship with You.

23

THE FRUIT OF
THE SPIRIT

*Walk in the Spirit, and you shall not fulfill
the lust of the flesh. For the flesh lusts against
the Spirit, and the Spirit against the flesh;
and these are contrary to one another, so
that you do not do the things that you wish.
But if you are led by the Spirit, you are not
under the law. . . . The fruit of the Spirit
is love, joy, peace, longsuffering, kindness,
goodness, faithfulness, gentleness, self-
control. Against such there is no law.*
GALATIANS 5:16–18, 22–23

Which one of us is as kind as we want to be? Or as patient? Who among us doesn't struggle with self-control or feel annoyed more often than loving? Now imagine the witness for Jesus we'd be if we consistently lived with joy and peace. But such traits do not come naturally. Instead, as the apostle Paul wrote, those traits are the fruit of the Holy Spirit, who lives within those who follow Jesus.

In Galatians 5 Paul also listed acts of the flesh that come all too easily and naturally. None of us needs a list to know what such actions are. If we simply read the headlines and look in the mirror, we'll be able to get quite a list going. But our gracious God doesn't leave us stuck in the flesh. Instead, as the Holy Spirit makes us more like Jesus, He brings forth the fruit of His presence.

I hope you are blessed by friends who walk in the Spirit, who enjoy a sweet relationship with Jesus, and who live with a winsome sense of contentment. These godly people make me want to lean into the Spirit so that my life displays more of His love, joy, peace, long-suffering, patience, kindness, goodness, faithfulness, gentleness, and self-control.

I praise You, Lord, for the fruit of Your Spirit. Please help me yield more fully to the Spirit's transforming work and to enjoy the contentment that comes with knowing His presence with me.

24

DOING GOOD

Let us not grow weary while doing good, for in due season we shall reap if we do not lose heart. Therefore, as we have opportunity, let us do good to all, especially to those who are of the household of faith.
GALATIANS 6:9–10

What actions come to mind when you think of "doing good"?

Opportunities to do good abound. People struggling to find a job, pay the bills, or stock the pantry have concrete needs that we can help meet in a variety of ways. A greater number of people are spiritually needy and want to find friends, peace, hope, and purpose. God can use us, His people, to help meet these needs as well.

As we become attuned to the needs of our family, friends, coworkers, neighbors, and community, we can feel overwhelmed even before we ask God where He would have us serve. We can be weary before we start, but we can keep from growing weary when we turn to God for His guidance and strength.

He wants to fill us with His presence, which means that we who are naturally so full of ourselves need to get out of the way and surrender to God's guiding and empowering presence. He loves His children's "Here am I!" and He loves to use us not only to make His love more real to our brothers and sisters in Christ but also to win to Himself the lost sheep He puts in our path.

Let us consciously walk in the Spirit and allow God to lead us. Doing so will help us "not grow weary while doing good" and find contentment in being used by God.

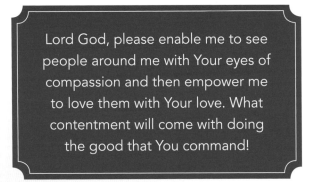

Lord God, please enable me to see people around me with Your eyes of compassion and then empower me to love them with Your love. What contentment will come with doing the good that You command!

25

PRESSING ON

*I press on, that I may lay hold of that for which
Christ Jesus has also laid hold of me. . . . One
thing I do, forgetting those things which are
behind and reaching forward to those things
which are ahead, I press toward the goal for the
prize of the upward call of God in Christ Jesus.*
PHILIPPIANS 3:12–14

By the time he wrote his letter to the Philippians, Paul had been unrelenting and effective in his work for his Lord. He had made three missionary journeys, teaching and preaching, planting churches and discipling younger church leaders. Yet as he wrote this letter from prison, Paul was still pressing "toward the goal for the prize of the upward call of God in Christ Jesus." What an example for us!

Are you reaching for the heavenly prize God has for you? Whatever kingdom work God has called you to, keep at it. You haven't crossed the finish line yet, so let me offer some encouragement:

1. *Believe and cling to God's promises.* Paul, for instance, lived with full confidence that God's indwelling Spirit would give him the power to fulfill his God-given potential in every area of life (Philippians 4:11).

2. *Focus on the precise goal God gives you.* God had called Paul to preach, and he was passionate about evangelizing the lost.

3. *Take courageous steps of faith, despite the possibility of failure.* Paul didn't let his weakness or fear deter him. He understood that God used his weakness and fear to keep him dependent on and strengthened by Christ (2 Corinthians 12:7–10).

What peace and contentment we'll know when, in the end, we can confidently say as Paul did, "I have fought the good fight, I have finished the race, I have kept the faith" (2 Timothy 4:7).

> May my Spirit-empowered efforts to fight the good fight give You glory, almighty God. I know that living to glorify You will bring a contentment that the world can't provide.

26

HAVING FAITH IN OUR FAITHFUL GOD

Now faith is the substance of things hoped for, the evidence of things not seen. . . . Without faith it is impossible to please Him, for he who comes to God must believe that He is, and that He is a rewarder of those who diligently seek Him.
HEBREWS 11:1, 6

Faith is the conviction that God will do what He has promised. Having faith means choosing to put our trust in our promise-keeping God and in His unlimited ability to do things we can't do. Of course our choice to believe in God pleases Him. After all, He created us to be in an intimate relationship of love, hope, and trust with Him.

As the basis of this relationship, our faith is an essential aspect of our Christian walk. In Scripture, we find examples of people who trusted God and people who didn't, and we undoubtedly see a bit of ourselves in each of these stories. It's good to know that our gracious God responds when we declare, "Lord, I believe; help my unbelief" (Mark 9:24). Even when our faith wavers, our faithful God doesn't.

Once we put our faith in Jesus, trusting in His forgiveness and love, we can be confident that a wonderful home in heaven awaits us. Until then, we can rely on Him, our Good Shepherd, to guide us through every set of circumstances we encounter in this life. Then, once we're at home with our heavenly Father, we will experience no more pain, and we will shed no more tears. We will know a heavenly contentment far greater than the mere tastes of contentment that this world offers.

Thank You for the gift of faith and for steadying me when I wobble. Thank You, too, for the contentment I can know this side of heaven when I, with a mustard seed of faith, choose to trust You.

27

THE WORLD WATCHES

We then who are strong ought to bear with the scruples of the weak, and not to please ourselves. Let each of us please his neighbor for his good, leading to edification. . . . May the God of patience and comfort grant you to be like-minded toward one another, according to Christ Jesus, that you may with one mind and one mouth glorify the God and Father of our Lord Jesus Christ. Therefore receive one another, just as Christ also received us, to the glory of God.

ROMANS 15:1–2, 5–7

What if someone could watch the members of your church do life for a while—beyond your interactions on Sunday mornings? Maybe they could watch you work together to develop a ministry, plan a program, sponsor a special event, and keep prayer requests confidential. From their observations, do you think they would know that you are Jesus' disciples? Would they see you love one another?

In John 13:35, Jesus taught that our love for one another is to be the reason that "all will know that you are My disciples." And the Lord commands us to love our brothers and sisters in Christ the way we want to be loved. Are we mature enough to love our annoying brother or the hard-to-love sister?

We will know contentment as we live according to the Lord's guidelines. Obeying His call to love means letting go of self-centered desires, surrendering more fully to God, and asking Him to help us love people with His love. Then the watching world will know we are Christians—and to God be the glory!

Thank You, God, for the ways You have loved me through Your people. Please use me to love others with Your love, so I can rest content knowing that the world can see that I am Yours.

28

WITHSTANDING TEMPTATION

Blessed is the man who endures temptation; for when he has been approved, he will receive the crown of life which the Lord has promised to those who love Him. Let no one say when he is tempted, "I am tempted by God"; for God cannot be tempted by evil, nor does He Himself tempt anyone.
JAMES 1:12–13

et me first reiterate what James said: God is never the source of the temptations we face in this life. Saying that God tempts us to sin is to confuse God with the devil.

May that truth come immediately to mind when we are tempted to do or say something that would not honor our God. And may that immediate remembrance compel us to grab the sword of the Spirit—God's Word—and do battle against our Enemy.

Of course Satan wants to draw us away from God and from the path of life He has outlined for us. But we can win this battle! Along with His living example, Jesus has given us His Spirit and the armor of God to help us with the Enemy's attacks. When Satan tempted Jesus by inaccurately using Scripture, Jesus responded with an accurately used biblical truth that enabled Him to stand strong. And after three rounds, Satan left Jesus alone (see Matthew 4:1–11).

Satan wants us to doubt God's goodness, faithfulness, and power so that we turn away from Him. That was his approach when he tempted Adam and

Eve: he wanted them to leave behind the life of perfect contentment God had designed for them, so he got them to question God's motives and love. Satan's strategy hasn't changed.

So whatever temptation you encounter, depend on the Holy Spirit and truth from the Bible for strength.

Holy Spirit, thank You for helping me recognize the Deceiver's lies when he tries to rob me of contentment by tempting me to greed, jealousy, and self-centeredness. Thank You for helping me stand strong!

29

ONLY FROM ABOVE

Who is wise and understanding among you? Let him show by good conduct that his works are done in the meekness of wisdom. . . . Where envy and self-seeking exist, confusion and every evil thing are there. But the wisdom that is from above is first pure, then peaceable, gentle, willing to yield, full of mercy and good fruits, without partiality and without hypocrisy.
JAMES 3:13, 16–17

Knowledge and wisdom are related, but they are definitely not the same. *Knowledge* is the collection of information we acquire; *wisdom* is using that knowledge in constructive, helpful ways. We can find knowledge in a multitude of places—lectures, textbooks, conversations, explorations of the world around us, and, yes, the internet—but genuine, life-giving wisdom comes from only one source: "The LORD gives wisdom" (Proverbs 2:6).

No wonder James instructed us, "If any of you lacks wisdom, let him ask of God, who gives to all liberally and without reproach, and it will be given to him" (James 1:5). And no wonder James's description of people who share this wisdom includes words like *meekness*, *peaceable*, and *willing to yield*.

A person sharing divine wisdom will speak with meekness and humility. God wants His representatives to have a gentle spirit when they speak with others, including brothers and sisters in Christ.

But God cares not only about how we deliver His wisdom but also how we receive it. He wants us to value wisdom as "better than rubies" (Proverbs

8:11), and He wants us to be teachable, to follow the "right paths" for life that His wisdom presents (Proverbs 4:11). And, yes, these paths lead to contentment.

So may we both humbly share the wisdom God calls us to speak, and may we humbly receive His wisdom when we hear it spoken.

> Lord, please help me recognize Your wisdom, share it when You call me to, and always walk according to it, blessed by Your presence with me, a presence that brings soul-satisfying contentment.

30

WHOM WILL
YOU SERVE?

*Now therefore, fear the L*ORD*, serve Him in sincerity and in truth, and put away the gods which your fathers served on the other side of the River and in Egypt. Serve the L*ORD*! And if it seems evil to you to serve the L*ORD*, choose for yourselves this day whom you will serve. . . . As for me and my house, we will serve the L*ORD.*

JOSHUA 24:14–15

et me share a Bible study tip: whenever you see the word *therefore*, ask yourself, "What is the *therefore* there for?" The answer is key to understanding the passage.

In this scripture, Joshua had reminded the people of Israel of their history: the plagues in Egypt, the parting of the Red Sea, and the crumbled walls of Jericho. What a powerful testimony to God's great faithfulness!

Joshua then continued, "*Therefore*, in light of God's faithfulness to you, whom will you serve?" He was essentially asking the Israelites, "Will you choose the one true God, or will you choose from among the many options the culture offers?" These questions are just as relevant to us today as they were to the tribes of Israel.

What other gods are we perhaps serving unintentionally? What does your calendar show to be the most important activity in your life? What possessions and relationships compete with your serving God? Where does growing your relationship with Him rank in your list of priorities?

In this life, we can find genuine contentment

only when we make our relationship with Jesus Christ our top priority. So may our heartfelt cry be that of the Israelites: "The LORD our God we will serve, and His voice we will obey!" (v. 24).

Thank You that Your Word offers me both a mirror and a compass. Scripture helps me recognize false gods I'm serving and directs me on the path of contentment that comes when Jesus is my top priority.

31

STAYING FOCUSED ON GOD

"This Book of the Law shall not depart from your mouth, but you shall meditate in it day and night, that you may observe to do according to all that is written in it. For then you will make your way prosperous, and then you will have good success. Have I not commanded you? Be strong and of good courage; do not be afraid, nor be dismayed, for the LORD your God is with you wherever you go."
JOSHUA 1:8–9

After Moses' death, the Lord Himself commissioned Joshua to lead the children of Israel. As He did so, the Almighty promised to be with Joshua as He had been with Moses: "No man shall be able to stand before you all the days of your life" (Joshua 1:5).

Our Creator God knows the nature of the human beings He created. He understands that trusting this promise becomes harder for us when we face the Enemy. So God didn't stop with just this rock-solid promise. Wanting to keep Joshua's courage from wavering, God called this new leader to stay focused on Him. And one of the best ways to do that—for Joshua and for us—is to meditate on the Word of God every day, morning and evening.

When a problem looms, we naturally find it easier to focus on that problem instead of on God. The Lord's promise "I will be with you. I will not leave you nor forsake you" (v. 5) is easier to believe when we read and remember His great faithfulness in His Word.

Our trust in God grows as we meditate on His Word and get to know Him better. We can also know the contentment that comes with living according to His will as we discover it in Scripture.

The world's noise and busyness can keep me from being heart-focused on You, my Savior and Lord, my Shepherd and Friend. I want to walk with You, being blessed by Your companionship and content in Your presence.

32

LOVING WITH CHRISTLIKE LOVE

Rejoice with those who rejoice, and
weep with those who weep. . . .
"If your enemy is hungry, feed him;
If he is thirsty, give him a drink;
For in so doing you will heap
coals of fire on his head."

Do not be overcome by evil, but
overcome evil with good.
ROMANS 12:15, 20–21

One way the followers of Jesus shine His light is by loving people in ways that reflect how Jesus Himself loved. And He loved people selflessly and sacrificially.

For instance, today's call to "rejoice with those who rejoice, and weep with those who weep" asks us to die to our natural self-centeredness. It is so much easier to be aware of our own feelings than other people's feelings. It is so much easier to indulge our joy or sadness than it is to set aside our emotions and increase another person's joy by joining in the celebration, or to lighten another person's pain by sharing in it. This kind of selfless love is Christlike love.

Christlike love is also sacrificial. And loving our enemy—and even our friends—by providing food and drink is indeed sacrificial. We'd much rather tend to our own meals or perhaps splurge on a meal with friends than feed a hungry enemy. But God commands us to kill 'em with kindness, to win them over with grace and generosity, to "overcome evil with good." Doing so will cost us financially, and it may require us to humble ourselves before people who have hurt, attacked, or somehow made life difficult for us. But we will know contentment as we act in costly obedience.

And we will shine God's light as we love like Jesus.

Loving like Jesus loves is a tall and even costly order, yet I know contentment comes when I obey Your commands. Please empower me to obey and use me to shine the light of Jesus' love in this dark world.

33

HELPER, TEACHER, COMFORTER— AND MORE!

Search me, O God, and know my heart;
Try me, and know my anxieties;
And see if there is any wicked way in me,
And lead me in the way everlasting.
PSALM 139:23–24

The Holy Spirit is the least understood person of the Trinity, yet He has so much to offer every follower of Jesus. For starters, consider that Jesus Himself referred to the Spirit as our "Helper" (John 14:26). And the kind of help the Spirit provides is invaluable. He helps us understand Scripture, teaches us God's truth, and enables us to call it to mind when we're sharing the gospel. The Spirit gives us wisdom so we can live according to the biblical truths He teaches. He offers guidance when we face decisions, strength when we're feeling overwhelmed by life, and comfort when we're saddened, hurt, or grieving.

And the list goes on. He also helps us by convicting us of our sin and by showing "any wicked way" in us so we can get back on track and follow His leading "in the way everlasting." We can get so comfortable with our sin that we fail to recognize that our words or actions are falling short of God's standards. Also, the Holy Spirit prays for you, and that's especially encouraging when we're at a loss: "We do not know what we should pray for . . . but the Spirit Himself makes intercession for us with groanings which cannot be uttered" (Romans 8:26).

So rely on the Spirit as you face the challenges of life. Let Him be your Helper, just as Jesus said. Walking with the Spirit will bring inner joy, peace, and contentment whatever life's circumstances.

> You, Holy Spirit, are Helper, Teacher, Comforter, Guide, Wisdom, Intercessor, and more. Thank You for making my heart Your home and blessing me with contentment and peace as we journey together.

34

JESUS WINS

"O Death, where is your sting?
O Hades, where is your victory?" . . .

Thanks be to God, who gives us the
victory through our Lord Jesus Christ.

Therefore, my beloved brethren, be steadfast,
immovable, always abounding in the work of
the Lord, knowing that your labor is not in vain.
1 CORINTHIANS 15:55, 57–58

Death can do much more than sting: it shatters hearts, destroys dreams, and fractures families. The darkness and hopelessness can suffocate and immobilize. In addition, senseless tragedies, rudderless living in this postmodern age, an arrogant sense of entitlement, self-destructive addictions—many aspects of life in a fallen world populated completely by sinners create hell on earth and a living death for many. *But God!*

But God intervened. He sent His Son to save us from sin, death, and hell. Jesus' sacrificial death on the cross was not the end of the rescue mission. Three days later Jesus rose from the dead, Conqueror of sin and death and Victor over hell. Jesus' victory ensures our own over sin and death, and we will celebrate that victory for eternity in heaven with Him. How marvelous that will be!

We are so blessed to have a wonderful Savior who willingly laid down His life so we could have life forever. And that sweet, eternal life with Jesus starts now as we walk with God through each day, trusting His guidance and provision, listening and learning, and enjoying His companionship. Our gracious God showers us with blessings and gives us peace that passes understanding, along with contentment in Him that defies life's circumstances.

Jesus' victory over sin and death means we win too.

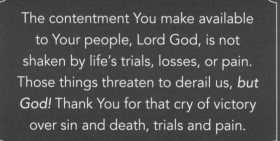

The contentment You make available to Your people, Lord God, is not shaken by life's trials, losses, or pain. Those things threaten to derail us, *but God!* Thank You for that cry of victory over sin and death, trials and pain.

35

WHY LOOK
ANYWHERE ELSE?

"Fear not, for I am with you;
Be not dismayed, for I am your God.
I will strengthen you,
Yes, I will help you,
I will uphold you with My righteous right hand."
ISAIAH 41:10

When I read a few verses earlier in Isaiah 41, I can almost picture God shaking His head. He had watched a goldsmith working at his anvil, then soldering the gold pieces together, and finally fastening his object with pegs so that this idol "might not totter" (Isaiah 41:7). What kind of hope can anyone find in a lowercase-*g* god that had to be propped up so that it wouldn't fall over? What kind of hope can we find in the twenty-first-century equivalent of that goldsmith's creation?

Perhaps more to the point, why would any of us—then or today—look for hope and help anywhere but the promise-making God of Isaiah 41:10? Look again at His pledge to be with us. He promises to be our God, to strengthen us, help us, and uphold us. Those promises of God offer us safety and security. And even more significant, those promises are God's declarations of His love for us.

Why would we look anywhere else for protection from our fears, for encouragement in the face of all that brings dismay, for strength when we are weak, or for help when we are in need? We should look no further than our good, powerful, faithful, and gracious God whose love for us will endure forever.

So rest in those truths. And find contentment in the 24/7 presence of your God.

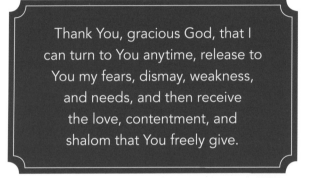

Thank You, gracious God, that I can turn to You anytime, release to You my fears, dismay, weakness, and needs, and then receive the love, contentment, and shalom that You freely give.

36

A HEART OF FLESH

"I will take you from among the nations, gather you out of all countries, and bring you into your own land. Then I will sprinkle clean water on you, and you shall be clean; I will cleanse you from all your filthiness and from all your idols. I will give you a new heart and put a new spirit within you; I will take the heart of stone out of your flesh and give you a heart of flesh."
EZEKIEL 36:24–26

Scattered throughout the ancient world, God's people, Israel, had not been good advertisements for their Lord, yet He remained faithful to them. Rather than washing His hands of them, God spoke of a future when He would gather all His people, cleanse them from their sinfulness, and "give [them] a new heart and put a new spirit within [them]."

What a gift! We all know the struggle to change, to become the better person we want to be—and that goal is much lower than being the person God created each one of us to be! Yet here we read of the new heart God has for us. He will fill us with His Spirit and with a desire to follow Him. This new heart is not merely a remodel; it's more of a tear-down and start-fresh construction project. God wants our new hearts to be characterized by our genuine desire to do His will and to live each moment in intimate relationship with Him.

By the power of His Spirit, our heart—hardened by sin and our lack of confession, and therefore having no experience of God's forgiveness—will again be tender toward God, yielded to His ways, filled with love for Him, and content in His good care. Great is God's faithfulness to us less-than-faithful human beings!

Lord God, I am well aware of how hard-hearted I can be. Thank You for not leaving me there, for instead softening my heart and moving me to a place where I can know contentment in You.

37

CHOOSING THE
SHADOW OF
GOD'S WINGS

Your mercy, O LORD, is in the heavens;
Your faithfulness reaches to the clouds.
Your righteousness is like the great mountains;
Your judgments are a great deep;
O LORD, You preserve man and beast.
How precious is Your lovingkindness, O God!
PSALM 36:5–7

What is your heart's response to these praise-filled words of David? His genuine joy is contagious! It's hard to do anything but join him in celebrating our amazing and wonderful God who, in His great mercy, forgives our sins, preserves our life, and blesses us with His loving-kindness. The only logical response to our good and gracious God is for "the children of men [to] put their trust under the shadow of [His] wings" (v. 7).

Yet we too often turn away from Him. "In Your light we see light," David proclaimed (v. 9), yet we too readily choose independence from God, despite the fact that He loves us with an everlasting love. We find ourselves wandering off His narrow path and into the ways of the world, straying from His light into the world's darkness.

Thankfully, He always shows us mercy: He welcomes us back when we acknowledge our turning away, our wanderings, our straying, our sin. Forgiven and cleansed, with our sin removed from us "as far as the east is from the west" (Psalm 103:12), we can rest in God's love. We can return to the shadow of His wings and know the blessing of contentment rooted in our precious relationship with Him. And may He get the glory for these gifts He so generously bestows!

> The truth that "You preserve man" comes to life as I imagine being hidden in the shadow of Your wings, protected from my enemies, and content in Your presence. I agree with the psalmist: "How precious is Your lovingkindness!"

38

CONTENTMENT NOW OR FOR ETERNITY?

"The hour has come that the Son of Man should be glorified. Most assuredly, I say to you, unless a grain of wheat falls into the ground and dies, it remains alone; but if it dies, it produces much grain. He who loves his life will lose it, and he who hates his life in this world will keep it for eternal life. If anyone serves Me, let him follow Me; and where I am, there My servant will be also. If anyone serves Me, him My Father will honor."
JOHN 12:23–26

Riding on a donkey, Jesus had entered Jerusalem to shouts of "Hosanna!" and the waving of palm branches. This note of celebration would soon take an ominous turn. Jesus reminded His disciples that He would soon die—a grain of wheat falling into the ground—in order to rise victorious over sin and death and thereby produce "much grain": the salvation of countless souls for eternity.

Besides earning us forgiveness of sin and eternal victory over death, Jesus was modeling a paradoxical truth for how to live. If we love all that the world offers us, we will lose everything that, right now, seems so important and valuable. However, if we live with our eyes on the Lord, we will know life for eternity. And eternal life with our Savior and Lord will be more satisfying than anything the world offers.

Are you living for the accomplishments, acquisitions, and acclaim the world offers? Living for those things can mean neglecting your soul. We pay the price for eternity when we do so.

The world offers only fleeting contentment. The

choice to nurture our souls and live according to God's kingdom priorities will mean contentment now and for eternity. Don't miss out!

Thank You that knowing You, Jesus, as my Savior and Lord brings contentment in this world and for eternity. When people notice the peace and joy I have in You, enable me to clearly share the gospel with them.

39

LIFE-GIVING WISDOM

My son, give attention to my words;
Incline your ear to my sayings.
Do not let them depart from your eyes;
Keep them in the midst of your heart;
For they are life to those who find them,
And health to all their flesh.
PROVERBS 4:20–22

The wisdom of Proverbs is just as relevant and essential today as it was when it was penned three thousand years ago. Each one of us twenty-first-century followers of Jesus would do well to "give attention" to the wisdom of God's Word and to "incline [our] ear" to its life-giving truth. The Lord—our Good Shepherd—longs to guide us, but are we listening for His voice?

In John 6:63 our Shepherd said, "The words that I speak to you are spirit, and they are life." The wisdom of Scripture gives physical life: our obedience protects us from sin and frees us from the bodily impact of unconfessed sin. This biblical wisdom also gives spiritual life: our obedience means a closer walk with Jesus, the Lover of our soul; a greater sensitivity to the Spirit's presence with and within us; and the blessed experience of God's pleasure with us as we live to glorify Him.

Finally, in a day noisy with voices vying for our attention online and off, we must train ourselves to keep our eyes on Jesus. The mind is the fountain from which our actions spring. If the fountain is pure, the stream that flows from it will be pure. So as a person thinks, so are they—a fact that underscores the importance of a God-focused thought life.

As we look to Jesus, He enables us to walk the path of holiness. As we follow His well-ordered ways, we will know joy and contentment in Him.

Thank You, God, for Your Word. May its timeless truth continue to enable me to know the contentment of walking closely with Jesus, focused on Him, guided by Your Spirit, and giving You glory.

40

GOD WILL BE GRACIOUS

Therefore the LORD will wait, that
He may be gracious to you;
And therefore He will be exalted,
that He may have mercy on you.
For the LORD is a God of justice;
Blessed are all those who wait for Him. . . .
He will be very gracious to you
at the sound of your cry;
When He hears it, He will answer you.
ISAIAH 30:18–19

As we encounter two instances of *therefore* in this scripture, let's remember to ask ourselves, What is the *therefore* there for?

First, God has just described Israel's unfounded confidence in Egypt and their rebellious disregard of His Word, His ways, and His longing for them to return to Him. Because the children of Israel have turned their back on God and walked away, He said, "Therefore I will wait."

Despite Israel's—and our—straying, the Lord wants to be gracious. He will wait until the disaster of our choices has taught us the foolishness of our ways, and He will be gracious. He can't *not* be gracious: grace is an aspect of His unchanging nature.

And whenever Israel—and we—return to God and receive His abundant grace, *therefore* God "will be exalted." His steadfast love and faithfulness to His people bring Him glory. He is recognized and exalted as King of kings when He blesses His people with mercy and grace. Those blessings come to us as He teaches us, guides us, forgives us, and redeems whatever we have done to dishonor our heavenly

Father. Rest assured that "He will be very gracious to you at the sound of your cry."

What a wonderful Savior is Jesus, our gracious Lord who guides our life for our good, our contentment, and His glory.

> Gracious God, please show me what unworthy thing I'm trusting in so that I can turn away from it and toward You for forgiveness. Only then will I know the contentment that comes with living for Your glory.

41

A TEMPLE OF THE HOLY SPIRIT

Do you not know that your body is the temple of the Holy Spirit who is in you, whom you have from God, and you are not your own? For you were bought at a price; therefore glorify God in your body and in your spirit, which are God's.

1 CORINTHIANS 6:19–20

t's another way those of us who follow Jesus are different from the world: we don't think of our body as our own. We acknowledge with the psalmist that God "created my inmost being . . . knit me together in my mother's womb. . . . I am fearfully and wonderfully made" (Psalm 139:13–14 NIV). We believers also know the truth of Genesis 1:26: "God said, 'Let Us make man in Our image, according to Our likeness.'"

As if being knit together by God and created in His image doesn't give us value enough, we also see in the New Testament how greatly God esteems the human body: "The Word became flesh and dwelt among us" (John 1:14). Furthermore, Christ paid for our salvation with His own body when He died an excruciating death on the cross. And we should always remember that we belong to Him who died, who rose again, and who gave us the gift of the Holy Spirit—and our body is a temple for Him to live within us.

May these truths from Scripture compel us to take care of our body, to honor God by not participating in ungodly activities, and to be humbled that Jesus—the Source of our contentment—dwells within us. Awestruck, may we bow before our almighty Creator God, yielding to His will and His ways.

Lord, thank You for Your Spirit who brings guidance, contentment, comfort, and peace. Please help me to take good care of my body as a response of gratitude for Your Spirit's indwelling and empowering presence.

42

SHINING AS LIGHTS

Work out your own salvation with fear and trembling; for it is God who works in you both to will and to do for His good pleasure.

Do all things without complaining and disputing, that you may become blameless and harmless, children of God without fault in the midst of a crooked and perverse generation, among whom you shine as lights in the world.
PHILIPPIANS 2:12–15

I f the beginning of today's passage is a little puzzling, let me reassure you that "by grace you have been saved through faith, and that not of yourselves; it is the gift of God, not of works, lest anyone should boast" (Ephesians 2:8–9). The command to "work out your own salvation" complements that profound truth. By grace, your salvation has been accomplished: Jesus did that work when He died on the cross as payment for your sin.

Once we receive that gift by believing the risen Jesus defeated sin and death, we "work out [our] own salvation" by investing in our relationship with Him. We choose various disciplines of the Christian life—Bible reading and study, Scripture memorization, worship, prayer, fellowship with believers—in order to grow in our faith and, by God's grace, in Christlikeness as well. We practice these disciplines "with fear and trembling," with awe, humility, and gratitude for the privilege of being in relationship with almighty God and adopted into His family.

As our words and actions reflect Jesus, as we love people with His love, and as we live with a sometimes-counterintuitive contentment, we "shine as lights in the world." Since light is always brighter against a dark background, we can shine quite brightly against the very dark backdrop our lost world offers. As Jesus said, "Let your light so shine" (Matthew 5:16)!

> My choices to complain and dispute rob me of the contentment You offer me. Please help me to instead live with humility and gratitude, working out my salvation and shining the light of Your love.

43

HUMBLED SERVANT, GLORIOUS LORD

*Christ Jesus, who, being in the form of God,
did not consider it robbery to be equal with
God, but made Himself of no reputation,
taking the form of a bondservant, and coming
in the likeness of men. And being found in
appearance as a man, He humbled Himself
and became obedient to the point of death,
even the death of the cross. Therefore God
also has highly exalted Him and given Him
the name which is above every name, that at
the name of Jesus every knee should bow.*

PHILIPPIANS 2:5–10

What an amazing passage, this ancient hymn of the early church! May we find ourselves awestruck by the humility of God's beloved Son. Jesus willingly descended from the glory of heaven to reside in a human body and to experience an excruciating death on a Roman cross in order to save our guilty souls. In perfect obedience to His Father, Jesus followed the divine plan of salvation designed by the Almighty before time began. This perfect obedience was at the same time an act of sacrificial love for wayward humanity.

Some of us recognize Jesus' life, death, and resurrection for what it is: the means of salvation from eternal separation from God. Yet this passage promises that one day every knee will bow before the risen and reigning King Jesus and recognize Him as Lord. Living in that sacred knowledge now brings—among many—the blessing of contentment. All praise to Him whose name is above every name!

I praise You that I already know to bow before You, the risen and reigning King Jesus. May that knowledge fuel contentment in this life as well as a fiery passion for sharing the gospel.

44

THE ALPHA AND THE OMEGA

"Behold, I am coming quickly, and My reward is with Me, to give to every one according to his work. I am the Alpha and the Omega, the Beginning and the End, the First and the Last. . . .

"I am the Root and the Offspring of David, the Bright and Morning Star."

And the Spirit and the bride say, "Come!" And let him who hears say, "Come!"
REVELATION 22:12–13, 16–17

The book of Revelation is a genre we're not used to, with its images that defy the imagination and events that have puzzled biblical scholars for centuries. The ultimate message is simple, though: Jesus wins. In the culminating event of that reality, He will return to earth as the conquering King and gather His faithful into the new heaven and new earth.

Consider the names our resurrected Lord—victorious over sin and death—used when He referred to Himself in these few verses describing His glorious return. He is, for instance, the *Alpha*, the first letter of the Greek alphabet, and the *Omega*, the last letter. Also by calling Himself "the Beginning and the End, the First and the Last," Jesus was declaring that He who co-created all that has been created will be the One to draw the curtain on this terrestrial stage of time.

No one knows the day or the hour when Jesus will return, but we who call Him "Savior" and "Lord" can experience the unshakable contentment that comes with knowing we're on the winning team. And it's not too late to confess your sin and accept Jesus as your Savior and Lord. Then you'll be on the winning team too.

> Thank You, Jesus, that You win! You will prove ultimately and eternally victorious over sin and death, a truth that means unshakable contentment for those of us who follow You.

45

A LIFESTYLE OF PRAYER

*Rejoice always, pray without ceasing,
in everything give thanks; for this is the
will of God in Christ Jesus for you.*
1 THESSALONIANS 5:16–18

P ray without ceasing"? How would any of us get anything done?

Perhaps the question warrants a closer look at Paul's instruction. The apostle did not mean that we should walk around all day mumbling prayers. Rather, Paul was calling followers of Jesus—then and now—to live in a constant attitude of prayer while going about their daily lives.

That attitude of prayer, though, can take on many moods. In some moments we may be thanking God for a blessing we usually take for granted. We may cry to Him for help when we hear a siren or notice a homeless person. We may ask for help as we try to love the "hard to love" or take a step of faith in a new ministry.

On some days we will find ourselves praying more frequently and more easily than we do on other days. On one day our to-do list might distract us; on other days the list itself may prompt specific prayers. Whatever the day holds and however the planned and unexpected events unfold, we can—by God's grace and with some practice—have an attitude of prayer. When we develop that attitude, we respond with prayer when we suddenly face a challenge or encounter a difficulty. We don't even have to think about praying. We just find ourselves praying!

This lifestyle of prayer is one of the secrets to contentment. Walking with the Lord through the day and talking with Him along the way brings a genuine sense of peace.

It makes sense that contentment comes with prayer, with heartfelt, ongoing communication with You, Lord Jesus. Please grow in me a passion for prayer. May prayer become my default mode as I journey through life.

46

SERVING WITHOUT FEAR AND IN GOD'S POWER

Stir up the gift of God which is in you through the laying on of my hands. For God has not given us a spirit of fear, but of power and of love and of a sound mind.
2 TIMOTHY 1:6–7

It was not a calm night on the Sea of Galilee when Jesus set out to join His disciples, who were in a boat halfway to the other side. The Twelve were terrified to see a figure walking on water, but recognizing the "ghost" to be Jesus, Peter stepped onto the water to join his rabbi. But when he turned his attention away from Jesus and to the raging wind, Peter started to sink. Of course Jesus didn't hesitate to help when Peter cried, "Lord, save me!" (Matthew 14:22–33).

When we step out to minister in an area of Holy Spirit–giftedness, we can be fearful, especially if we are more aware of the circumstances than of Jesus' presence with us. We need the reminder that Paul gave Timothy: "God has not given us a spirit of fear, but of power and of love and of a sound mind." Fear is not of God, yet fear is a natural and often very appropriate response to circumstances. Yet living with a constant spirit of fear and timidity is counter to who we are in Jesus. Thanks to the indwelling Holy Spirit, we always have access to God's power and love.

Whenever we feel fearful, let's immediately ask

God to help us. Then, as we exercise our spiritual gift, we will be doing so in His strength. We'll also find that fear loses its grip when we step out with faith that He will empower us. What satisfaction and contentment come when we serve our God in His power!

> Good and gracious God, fear does not come from You, but contentment and strength and joy do. So please help me serve You and others in Your power and with a heart overflowing with Your love.

47

THE SWORD OF THE SPIRIT

All who desire to live godly in Christ Jesus will suffer persecution. But evil men and impostors will grow worse and worse, deceiving and being deceived. But you must continue in the things which you have learned and been assured of, knowing from whom you have learned them . . .

All Scripture is given by inspiration of God, and is profitable for doctrine, for reproof, for correction.
2 TIMOTHY 3:12–14, 16

Always a straight shooter, Paul taught that followers of Jesus will not avoid persecution, likely so that we would not be blindsided or perplexed when it happened. But Paul was confident that God's people would stand firm because we have at the ready "the sword of the Spirit, which is the word of God" (Ephesians 6:17).

Scripture prepares us for whenever and in whatever form the inevitable persecution comes. And God's people will be able to endure evil people, imposters, and deceivers when we rely on the truth and power of His written Word.

God also gave us His Word "for doctrine, for reproof, for correction, for instruction in righteousness." Scripture teaches us about God, corrects us when we are wrong, and instructs us in how to be effective Christians in the battle against evil.

In addition, we can find contentment when we place our confidence in the truth and power of God's Word. So may God bless us with a real hunger for His Word and with a steadfast commitment to wielding that sword of the Spirit with skill and effectiveness.

Thank You for the sword of Your Spirit, for Your inspired Word that teaches, corrects, and equips me for a life of good works and contented obedience. Enable me to wield the sword effectively on behalf of Truth.

48

GOD'S SAVING AND SANCTIFYING GRACE

*The grace of God that brings salvation
has appeared to all men, teaching us that,
denying ungodliness and worldly lusts, we
should live soberly, righteously, and godly in
the present age, looking for the blessed hope
and glorious appearing of our great God
and Savior Jesus Christ, who gave Himself
for us, that He might redeem us from every
lawless deed and purify for Himself His own
special people, zealous for good works.*
TITUS 2:11–14

When we, by faith, accept Jesus' death on the cross as payment for our sin, our salvation is, by God's grace, secured. Then we begin our process of sanctification, of our becoming more like Jesus. During this lifelong process, we can experience God's saving grace empowering us to daily crucify our worldly flesh, so that we might glorify Him in the way we live. In fact, when we make it our goal to live for God's glory, we will find ourselves living "soberly, righteously, and godly" and sinning less. (That goal of living to sin less, rather than living for God's glory, won't necessarily result in our glorifying God, because our focus will be too much on ourselves.)

Desiring to glorify God in all we do will lead us to do the good works of God, "to obey . . . to speak evil of no one, to be peaceable, gentle, showing all humility to all men" (Titus 3:1–2). Doing good works is not a way to salvation; doing good works is instead evidence of our gratitude for God's saving grace.

May we therefore be preoccupied with living for God's glory and sharing His glorious grace with others. Living that way pleases God, and pleasing Him brings us great contentment.

> Good and gracious God, please help me live for Your glory, not mine. Help me choose contentment instead of complaint and service instead of self-centeredness, so that one day I hear Your "Well done!"

49

ACCEPTANCE GUARANTEED

The word of God is living and powerful, and sharper than any two-edged sword. . . .

Seeing then that we have a great High Priest who has passed through the heavens, Jesus the Son of God, let us hold fast our confession. For we do not have a High Priest who cannot sympathize with our weaknesses, but was in all points tempted as we are, yet without sin. Let us therefore come boldly to the throne of grace, that we may obtain mercy and find grace to help in time of need.
HEBREWS 4:12, 14–16

nspired by the Spirit, God's written Word is a tool He uses for our sanctification. It pierces our thoughts and penetrates our heart, helping us recognize the ways we fall short of God's standards. We have no secrets from Him, and that truth sounds terrifying—but keep reading.

We are blessed that our High Priest—Jesus Himself—can "sympathize with our weaknesses." After all, He faced temptations to sin, but He never gave in. Jesus never sinned, but He knows what it is to struggle against temptation, and He wants to help. That's why we find this invitation to "come boldly to the throne of grace." We aren't to be fearful, timid, or worried about how He might respond to us. He has promised to provide us with mercy and grace "to help in time of need."

What peace and contentment we can find in this reassurance of our Savior's unwavering acceptance of us.

As familiar as a passage might be, Lord, Your written Word is always fresh and evergreen. Thank You that it is living and active, sanctifying, transforming, and guiding me along a path of contentment in You.

50

PRAYING FERVENTLY

Is anyone among you sick? Let him call for the elders of the church, and let them pray over him, anointing him with oil in the name of the Lord. And the prayer of faith will save the sick, and the Lord will raise him up. And if he has committed sins, he will be forgiven. Confess your trespasses to one another, and pray for one another, that you may be healed. The effective, fervent prayer of a righteous man avails much.

JAMES 5:14–16

Overwhelmed by life's circumstances? Immobilized by grief or fear? Stressed by all life is demanding? Losing hope as you wait for healing? We've all been there.

Rather than allowing ourselves to be victims of circumstances or passively waiting for circumstances to change, let's go to the Lord in prayer. Whatever the burden, let's earnestly approach our sovereign God with fervent and faith-filled prayer, rejoicing in good times and requesting guidance, provision, protection, or redemption in tough times.

God can and does heal, sometimes through modern medicine and sometimes with His direct touch—and to Him be the glory in both cases. God, however, hasn't promised to heal everyone in need, so we can't demand the gift of healing. And we might never understand when healing comes slowly or not at all, despite our ongoing and expectant prayers.

In those times, we choose to rest in the knowledge that God is good, merciful, gracious, loving, and wise—and always will be. May that truth be the solid foundation of our contentment: we choose to trust God despite His inscrutable ways, and we choose to trust Him to be sufficient for us even if our circumstances don't change. We fervently pray even as we humbly bow before Him.

> Lord God, I want to be a person who prays fervently, who prays specifics but who always humbly yields to Your will, and who chooses to be content however You respond to my most passionate prayers.

51

BEING HOLY AS
JESUS IS HOLY

*Gird up the loins of your mind, be sober, and
rest your hope fully upon the grace that is to
be brought to you at the revelation of Jesus
Christ; as obedient children, not conforming
yourselves to the former lusts, as in your
ignorance; but as He who called you is holy,
you also be holy in all your conduct, because
it is written, "Be holy, for I am holy."*
1 PETER 1:13–16

Our crucified and resurrected Jesus gives us hope, inheritance, and salvation. In response, we are to live purposefully, focusing on Jesus and growing in spiritual maturity.

Followers of the Lord are to be serious about becoming spiritually mature. We are to "gird up the loins of [our] mind." Just as a soldier tied up his ankle-length tunic so he could move more easily in battle, we are to pull in all the loose ends, all the random thoughts that fill our minds. We are to focus on God's grace that will ultimately be evident in the return of Christ.

"Girding up our mind" involves obeying God's commands, turning our back on sinful ways, and being holy in all we say and do. Being holy—living differently from our culture—reflects the reality of our salvation and honors God. The Bible teaches us about this holy life, and Jesus Himself models it for us. Just as Jesus did, we are to give our life in service to others, forgive those who sin against us, and love the hard to love. Every day we can make a difference in someone's life for the Lord.

Following Jesus' example—being holy as He

Himself is holy—won't be easy, but it is the path of obedience to God's will. It is, therefore, the path of contentment.

Obeying Your commands leads to contentment, Lord. So I ask You to help me to obey You. Please also enable me to be holy as You are holy, to love, to forgive, and to live differently from the world.

52

GOD'S GRACE FOR THE HUMBLE

"God resists the proud,
But gives grace to the humble."

Therefore humble yourselves under the
mighty hand of God, that He may exalt
you in due time, casting all your care
upon Him, for He cares for you.
1 PETER 5:5–7

In his book *The Purpose-Drive Life*, Rick Warren wisely observed, "Humility is not thinking less of yourself, but thinking of yourself less." That definition offers a nice backdrop for Peter's call to humble ourselves—to think less often about ourselves and more often about others, to be concerned not only about what is going on in our lives but also what the people around us are going through, to seek not to be served but to serve, and to get off the throne of our lives and yield to the kingship of God.

Now consider the promise for those of us who humble ourselves like that: God "gives grace to the humble." We will know God's grace—His unmerited favor—when we love Him with all we are, when we live in the truth that God is God and we are not, and when we begin each day saying, "Here am I, Lord. Send me!"

Our heavenly Father also wants us to humbly cast on Him all our worries and cares. He who has our best interest in mind doesn't want us to struggle alone. Jesus wants to walk with us as our Guide, our Comforter, our Helper, our Good Shepherd. Accept that invitation with heartfelt gratitude for His great love. As you humbly rely on the Holy Spirit and walk hand in hand with Jesus, our almighty God will lift you up so that you can live with contentment and joy.

Thank You, Almighty God, for caring for me. Thank You, Lord Jesus, for walking alongside me through life. Thank You, Holy Spirit, for providing strength, guidance, comfort, and contentment. I am humbled and grateful for this grace!

53

JOY DESPITE AFFLICTION

You became followers of us and of the Lord, having received the word in much affliction, with joy of the Holy Spirit, so that you became examples to all in Macedonia and Achaia who believe. . . . You turned to God from idols to serve the living and true God, and to wait for His Son from heaven, whom He raised from the dead, even Jesus who delivers us from the wrath to come.
1 THESSALONIANS 1:6–7, 9–10

Before you became a believer, did God put someone in your life whose relationship with Him was intriguing, even compelling? The faithfulness of God's people, especially during hard times, glorifies Him and draws people to Jesus.

The Lord's followers in Thessalonica offer us an example of faithfulness in hard times. They made the costly decision to turn from their idols and serve "the living and true God." They had "received the word in much affliction" yet with "joy of the Holy Spirit." They found joy in Jesus despite suffering for their new faith.

Throughout Scripture, we see God's people experiencing joy and even contentment in the midst of life's inevitable suffering (John 16:33). The Thessalonians were young in their faith, but Paul was greatly impressed by the way their example encouraged other believers. Thank God for people in your life who have modeled joy and contentment as they continued their "work of faith, labor of love, and patience of hope" despite real hardship. May the Lord use us in the same way.

When hard times come, Lord God,
please enable me to cling to You.
In those times, please use me to
shine with joy and contentment
in You despite my experience
of life's losses and pain.

54

TO GOD BE THE GLORY

Whether you eat or drink, or whatever you do, do all to the glory of God. Give no offense, either to the Jews or to the Greeks or to the church of God, just as I also please all men in all things, not seeking my own profit, but the profit of many, that they may be saved.
1 CORINTHIANS 10:31–33

n the early church, it was a big deal when Jewish followers of Jesus realized they no longer needed to follow their people's long-standing food laws. Now, rather than observing strict Levitical law, Jesus' followers could make decisions about what they ate. At the same time, however, these individuals were to "give no offense" as they enjoyed their new freedom; they were not to be stumbling blocks for fellow Jews who were still trying to get their mind around this sea change. Freely eating non-kosher food might either encourage or discourage the spiritual growth of fellow diners.

Aware of that fact, the apostle Paul wrote, "Whether you eat or drink, or whatever you do, do all to the glory of God," setting forth a principle for us today. Some Jesus followers today refrain from certain behaviors and activities. If we don't see biblical reason to avoid those things, let's enjoy them. But let's not enjoy them at the expense of the people around us. Our decision may make all the difference in someone else's Christian walk.

So ask God for guidance. Enjoy the freedom

you have in Jesus without being a stumbling block to others. Your peace and contentment in following Jesus the person rather than a code of law can be a compelling witness to the gospel. So in everything you say and do, "do all to the glory of God."

Lord, I want to "do all" to Your glory!
I don't want to draw attention to
myself or cause anyone to stumble.
Instead, may my contentment
in You be a winsome witness to
the freedom we have in You.

55

SHOWING GOD
OUR LOVE

*This is the love of God, that we
keep His commandments. And His
commandments are not burdensome.*
1 JOHN 5:3

When we recognize Jesus as the Son of God and accept Him as our Lord and Savior, we are taking the first step on the path to complete contentment. Knowing that we are loved by Jesus and now walking the path He has set forth for us can only lead to contentment—unless. . . .

When we try to obey God's commands in our own power, those commandments feel burdensome. As we stumble and fail to love God with all we are and as we stumble and fail to love people with God's gracious love, we can experience frustration and discouragement. Given our sinful nature, we will never—on our own—be able to love God wholeheartedly, and we will never find the ability to love others the way we ourselves want to be loved.

But we find great joy, freedom, and contentment when, relying on the Spirit of God to help us, we obey God's commands. After all, the Spirit is at work in us, making us more like Jesus. We see evidence of His work in the baby steps we take toward loving God more perfectly and people more generously.

Furthermore, let's remember that every command God has given is for our good: His call to forgive keeps us free from bitterness, and His command to serve others keeps us from self-centeredness. So may we appreciate the goodness of God's commandments and, in the power of His Spirit, demonstrate our love for our almighty heavenly Father by obeying those commands.

And as we walk this path and grow in Christlikeness, God will be glorified, and we will know greater contentment.

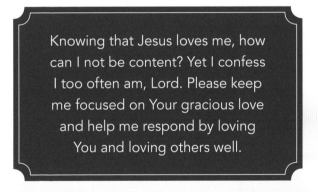

Knowing that Jesus loves me, how can I not be content? Yet I confess I too often am, Lord. Please keep me focused on Your gracious love and help me respond by loving You and loving others well.

56

GOD'S UNCHANGING COMMANDMENTS

I rejoiced greatly that I have found some of your children walking in truth, as we received commandment from the Father. And now I plead with you, lady, not as though I wrote a new commandment to you, but that which we have had from the beginning: that we love one another. This is love, that we walk according to His commandments. . . .

For many deceivers have gone out into the world who do not confess Jesus Christ as coming in the flesh. This is a deceiver and an antichrist.

2 JOHN 1:4–7

As he had stated elsewhere, John again said that we show our love for God when "we walk according to His commandments." And those commandments never change.

We find God's commandments in His written Word, and His truth is the same today and every day in the future. So we need to be students of Scripture to know God's way and be confident in our understanding of His commandments. That way, when a new teaching comes along, we will recognize it as the deceit that it is.

These are the greatest commandments: to love God with all we are—heart, soul, mind, and strength—and to love the people around us the way we want to be loved (Matthew 22:37–39). Again, those commandments have not changed and will not change.

But will you obey God's commandments? Will you walk your own path, or will you choose His way? Surrendering ourselves to God's will and choosing to walk through life holding His hand, we will know the contentment that comes with living the way our Creator designed us to live.

Thank You that Your love for me never changes, Lord God, and neither do Your commandments. Thank You for the peace and contentment that come when I obey Your consistent and trustworthy commands.

57

SINNERS SAVED
BY GRACE

I thank Christ Jesus our Lord . . . because
He counted me faithful, putting me into the
ministry, although I was formerly a blasphemer,
a persecutor, and an insolent man. . . . The
grace of our Lord was exceedingly abundant,
with faith and love which are in Christ Jesus.
1 TIMOTHY 1:12–14

n this description of himself, the apostle Paul was not overstating his case. Before becoming a follower of Jesus, he was a persecutor of the Lord's followers. Zealous for his beloved Judaism, Paul "made havoc of the church . . . dragging off men and women, committing them to prison" (Acts 8:3). But Paul met Jesus on the road to Damascus, and persecutor became preacher. He boldly preached the gospel message of grace and forgiveness. Paul passionately shared the truth that "Christ Jesus came into the world to save sinners, of whom I am chief" (1 Timothy 1:15).

If you feel guilty of a sin you think God cannot forgive, be encouraged by Paul's testimony. Only the Enemy—Satan, the deceiver and accuser—would have you believe that. Don't listen to him. Turn to the truth, which Paul's life exemplifies. God forgives every single one of our sins and removes them as far away from us as the east is from the west (Psalm 103:12). God has abundant grace for us, no matter how far we run from Him.

The simple truth is we are all sinners saved by God's grace. May we rest in God's saving grace, feel content in the security of Jesus' love, and freely share the gospel with others so that they, too, may know the contentment that comes with being welcomed into the family of God.

Lord God, I never want to take for granted Your saving grace, and I want to always be amazed by its abundance. Thank You for the contentment I find as You continually pour Your sustaining grace into my life.

58

THE FRAGRANCE
OF CHRIST

*Now thanks be to God who always leads us
in triumph in Christ, and through us diffuses
the fragrance of His knowledge in every place.
For we are to God the fragrance of Christ
among those who are being saved and among
those who are perishing. To the one we are
the aroma of death leading to death, and to
the other the aroma of life leading to life.*
2 CORINTHIANS 2:14–16

I f you need to be reminded of your purpose in life, today's verses are for you.

First, we can celebrate with Paul that God is with us, enabling us to be victorious over sin, to know His guidance, and to be His light in this dark world as we love the people around us with His love. The contentment that comes with such God-centered living does not go unnoticed.

In fact, God uses you and me and our counter-cultural ways for His kingdom: "God . . . diffuses the fragrance of His knowledge in every place." In some of those places, people who are being saved, as well as those who are perishing, notice us. Think for a moment: Is there something about you that offers a subtle fragrance of Jesus to people you encounter?

Consider Paul's example. Whenever he spent time with people, those individuals came to know Jesus better. As Paul lived and taught with passion, humility, and gratitude, he exhibited the unmistakable loveliness of the Master. God will use you in the same way, showcasing Jesus through the generosity, hospitality, joy, and contentment you display whatever life's circumstances.

By God's grace, you will be the sweet-smelling fragrance of Christ that attracts people to our good and gracious Savior Jesus.

Jesus, please help me live a God-centered life of contentment so that—like a flower's fragrance drawing attention to its source—I draw attention to You so that others come to recognize You as their Lord and Savior.

59

A STRIKING FAMILY RESEMBLANCE

Be kind to one another, tenderhearted, forgiving one another, even as God in Christ forgave you.

Therefore be imitators of God as dear children. And walk in love, as Christ also has loved us and given Himself for us, an offering and a sacrifice to God for a sweet-smelling aroma.
EPHESIANS 4:32–5:2

t's hard not to point out a family resemblance when you see it. "She looks a lot like her mother!" "He walks just like his dad does."

But what about a *spiritual* family resemblance? "They love just like their heavenly Father does."

Followers of Jesus aspire to this comparison as they live with kingdom values and goals. When we become children of God, we are to imitate our Father to such a degree that everyone sees with absolute certainty that we are our Father's children.

One reason we live like this is because "God in Christ forgave [us]." And the best way we could respond to that gift of love is by loving God and others.

Our choice to love is one way God intends for us to be light in a dark world, showing the way to spiritual safety for those about to sink in the depths of life. We have the privilege and responsibility of representing Jesus in this lost world. We love with our words and actions, always ready to "give a defense" to those who ask for the "reason for the hope that is in [us]" (1 Peter 3:15).

May our distinct way of loving people—believers

and nonbelievers alike—be such a striking family resemblance to our heavenly Father that people can't help but notice the similarity and want to know Him better. True contentment comes when God uses us like that.

Holy Spirit, continue to transform me so that I bear an ever-clearer family resemblance to my Lord Jesus. Enable me to represent Him well as, by Your grace, I live a winsome life of joy and contentment.

60

"I WILL GIVE YOU REST"

"Come to Me, all you who labor and are heavy laden, and I will give you rest. Take My yoke upon you and learn from Me, for I am gentle and lowly in heart, and you will find rest for your souls. For My yoke is easy and My burden is light."
MATTHEW 11:28–30

Life is hard. Disappointments, losses, derailed dreams, unrelenting illness, straying children, financial struggles—these are only some of the many burdens we can find ourselves carrying. And Jesus, who walked this earth, knows about the burdens of life. He saw firsthand the illness, grief, oppression, and brokenness that are part of the human condition. And He, our compassionate and gracious Savior, is the One issuing the invitation, "Come to Me . . . and I will give you rest."

With open arms, the Lord extends this lifelong invitation to each of us. He will provide the rest we need—the physical, spiritual, emotional, mental, and relational rest—whenever we let go of our burdens and release them to Him. Jesus will always refresh our weary souls.

But notice that Jesus didn't say anything about removing *all* our burdens or protecting us from *all* problems. Instead, He promised to be with us as we undergo trials, experience heartache, and feel worn down by the demands of everyday life. That means we'll never have to bear our very real burdens alone. We can choose to accept Jesus' invitation and be yoked with Him, the One who gives us sufficient grace whenever we turn to Him.

Take joy in this truth: your willingness to be yoked to Jesus and to let Him lift the burdens wearing you down will result in peace and contentment. After all, He promises, "You will find rest for your souls. For My yoke is easy and My burden is light."

I know I can't bear life's yokes on my own, I can't find rest apart from You, and I will never know life-giving contentment on my own. So, with gratitude, I turn to You for rest and to find contentment.

BEFORE YOU GO

"The LORD bless you and keep you;
The LORD make His face shine upon you,
And be gracious to you;
The LORD lift up His countenance upon you,
And give you peace."
NUMBERS 6:24–26

started this book by asking you to consider what brings you contentment. You may have different ideas at this point. You may even have a new definition of the word *contentment.*

God wants you to experience contentment in this life, but the contentment He offers is different from the world's sham offerings. God's path to contentment also differs from the world's.

The world promises us happiness, that feeling we experience because of certain favorable circumstances that won't last forever and that might not last for even five more minutes. Our happiness at work disappears when the boss retires. Our happiness in a friendship vanishes when that person finds a new best friend.

In addition to contentment-robbers like these, advertisers sow seeds of discontent in us before presenting their paths to happiness. Your house is fine, but a more prestigious neighborhood is opening up. Your car is reliable, but a new and improved model is now available.

Life's disappointments and the culture's shiny offerings can distract us, unsettle us, and make us wonder if we're missing out. That's when we need to remember that living in the love of Jesus is the secret to genuine contentment.

We learn about living in Jesus' love when we open the Bible and ask the Holy Spirit to show us. We see, for instance, that we are to welcome the Lord's correction, do the good that we're able to do, and live before the Lord with humility. In addition to teaching us how to live in a way that honors God, the Holy Spirit empowers us to apply those truths. After all, as you've read in these pages, in no other place than living according to God's will do we find real contentment.

The happiness the world offers is fleeting, but God offers an alternative: He longs to bless you with contentment that is rooted in His eternal truth, wisdom, and love. And it's yours to receive.

SCRIPTURE INDEX

ABOUT THE AUTHOR

Jack Countryman is the founder of JCountryman gift books, a division of Thomas Nelson, and is the recipient of the Evangelical Christian Publishers Association's Kip Jordan Lifetime Achievement Award. Over the past 30 years, he has developed bestselling gift books such as *God's Promises for Your Every Need*, *God's Promises for Men*, *God's Promises for Women*, *God Listens*, and *The Red Letter Words of Jesus*. Countryman's books have sold more than 27 million units. His graduation books alone have sold nearly 2 million units.

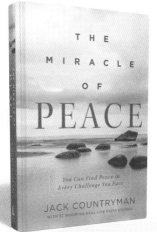
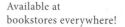

Some of the sons of Benjamin and Judah came to David at the stronghold. And David went out to meet them, and answered and said to them, "If you have come peaceably to me to help me, my heart will be united with you; but if to betray me to my enemies, since there is no wrong in my hands, may the God of our fathers look and bring judgment." Then the Spirit came upon Amasai, chief of the captains, and he said:

> *"We are yours, O David;*
> *We are on your side, O son of Jesse!*
> *Peace, peace to you,*
> *And peace to your helpers!*
> *For your God helps you."*

So David received them, and made them captains of the troop.

1 CHRONICLES 12:16–18

1

CHOOSING PEACE
WITH EACH OTHER

We've all had the experience of being in a conversation that gets more and more intense, and we reach a point when we aren't sure which way the conversation will go. Emotions encourage us to win the argument or return an insult for an insult. What if, instead, we chose to make peace with that brother or sister in Christ?

God's way is the way of peace. He also wants unity among His followers. When—by His grace—we get past how we feel and seek to be at peace with our brothers and sisters, we can experience a change of heart and possibly avoid saying or doing something we will regret in the future. So take to God in prayer whatever aspect of the conversation—or the person!—is bothering you. Listen for the Holy Spirit to be your guide and rely on Him to enable you to obey.

To settle or to avoid a conflict, first turn to God and seek His Spirit's guidance. God is always ready for us to come to Him with an open heart and mind. He is always ready to provide you with the wisdom you need (James 1:5).

REFLECTION

If you were to stop and listen for God the next time conflict arises, what might you expect to hear from Him?

Grace to you and peace [inner calm and spiritual well-being] from God our Father and the Lord Jesus Christ.

1 CORINTHIANS 1:3 AMP

2

PEACE FROM ABOVE

Three years ago—and one month after I had fallen and hit the side of my face—my wife, Marsha, and I were watching television. When I turned to her to speak, I couldn't utter a single word. When we called the doctor the next morning, the nurse told me to go to the local medical center immediately—and we did.

Discovering that I had blood on the brain, the doctor sent me to Vanderbilt, where I learned that I had three options: (1) wait and see if the blood was absorbed into my body; (2) have a craniotomy where they remove a portion of my skull and stop the bleeding; or (3) have a burr hole surgery where they drill one or more small holes in my head and use a tube to drain off the blood. Without hesitation, I decided to have the burr hole surgery. What amazes me is that I had no doubt or fear; I was completely at peace. Later, when I went into the hospital for the surgery, I had the same confidence that God was in charge and He would take care of me. And He did.

Two weeks after the surgery, I went to see my family doctor. He looked me in the eyes and asked, "Jack, do you know how lucky you are? Seven out of ten people die when they have blood on the brain."

As I think back on that entire situation, I realize I never feared for my life. Every step of the way, God gave me a sense of peace that I cannot explain. I had no doubt that He was with me and that I would come through the surgery just fine.

When you choose to turn your life over to God, the Holy Spirit within you becomes your Comforter (John 14:16 kjv). Praise God! What a blessing!

REFLECTION

Walk through—as I just did—a time in your life when you had to face fear head-on. Comment on the degree of peace you had or didn't have each step of the way.